souls

BENEATH AND BEYOND AUTISM

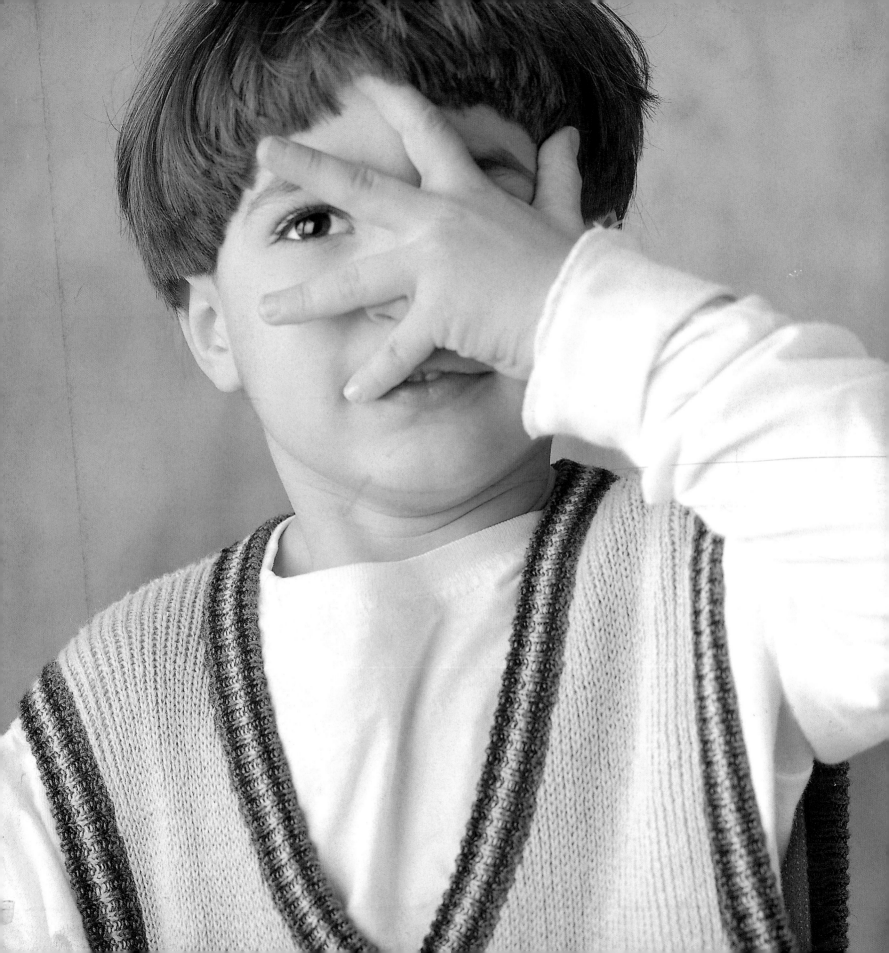

souls

BENEATH AND BEYOND AUTISM

Concept and photography by Thomas Balsamo

Written by Sharon Rosenbloom

SOULS: BENEATH AND BEYOND AUTISM

Published by McGraw-Hill, a business unit of The McGraw-Hill Companies, Inc., 1221 Avenue of the Americas, New York, NY 10020.

3 4 5 6 7 8 9 0 CCW/CCW 0 9 8 7 6

ISBN 0-07-7288170-4

Vice president: Craig Beytien
Production supervisor: Cheryl Horch
Concept and photography by: Thomas Balsamo
Writing: Sharon Rosenbloom
Design and composition: donated by Keith J. McPherson, WhiteOak Creative
Typeface: 13/28 Goudy
Printer: Quebecor World Eusey Press

Library of Congress Control Number: 2002116035

www.booksthattouch.com

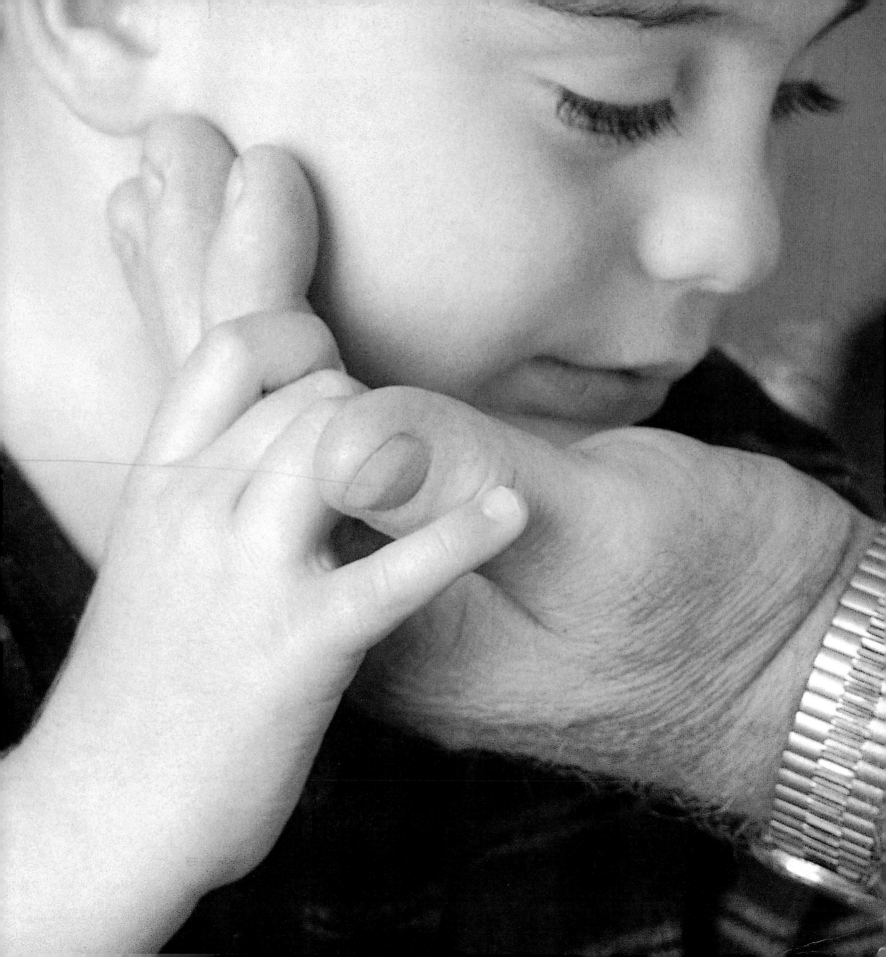

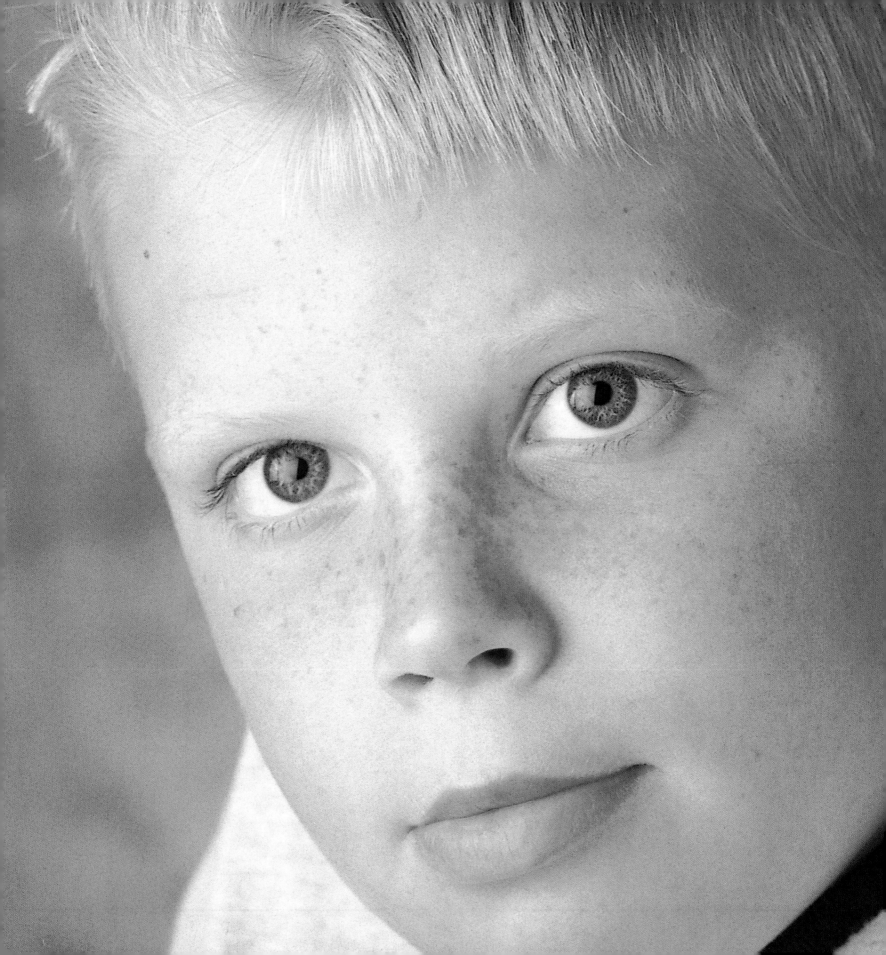

This book is dedicated to Joey Rosenbloom and those of us living and loving in the world of autism.

souls

This project is committed to portraying autism and, more profoundly, individuals with autism, from the inside out. Through the media of photography and writing, this book hopes to educate and inspire by breaking apart stereotypes associated with autism while showing vividly that love is omnipotent in our trials and triumphs.

Love is the ultimate lesson, weapon, and savior as we struggle to understand and overcome life's challenges each day.

The writing describes a journey, taking readers through hope, despair, pain and resurrection. It touches on the collective human experience of suffering and redemption while showing a pathway to a profoundly higher ground of understanding and acceptance.

The story is written from a collective heart, formed by countless intimate exchanges with families struggling and triumphing again and again as they live and love in the autistic world.

The greater purpose, beyond the story of autism, is the universal message that from the depths of darkness, often we find the greatest enlightenment. The autistic individual is a beautiful metaphor for this belief.

In a culture that bombards us with messages that perfection is the key to happiness, autistic individuals and their families dare to challenge this notion while drawing others to look beneath and beyond the superficial. With startling beauty, the images prove what in words alone might be denied: that beneath and beyond autism there is a reality often missed--a will, a soul, an identity that achieves the full measure of its creation -- to connect with others in ways not seen or appreciated by surface observation.

This combination of narrative and photography becomes a powerful parable that reaches and teaches far beyond autism itself, touching on spiritual truths often lost in the cultural mainstream.

... to connect
with others in ways not seen...

From the Heart of Thomas Balsamo

As a young man, I studied the life of Leonardo Da Vinci. His passion for using his gifts to leave a legacy to the world profoundly affected me. In that spirit, I sought to create a book that would benefit humanity.

I have studied portraiture since 1978 and strive to interpret, not merely photograph. I have been compelled to create images that capture the true essence of the human spirit rather than record only physical attributes. I was in search of a project that would challenge me to create portraits that glimpse the human soul. I hoped the work would contain a deeper universal message. I knew the opportunity would present itself when the time was right.

The wait ended in the summer of 1999 when Sharon commissioned me to create new portraits of her children, Joey and Raia. I had done work for Sharon and Bob several times before and knew Joey, a bright, friendly boy dealing with autism. For this portrait session, Sharon began to educate me about autism. She passionately explained how to connect with Joey during the session, to better capture his true self.

To reinforce to me how important these approaches were in connecting to autistic children, she shared her experiences with other families. Her passion and knowledge on the subject of autism made a strong impression on me. As she was leaving my studio she stated, "Someday I will write a book." I was unable to stop thinking about Sharon and our conversation, and I knew I had been called to help her get her message out. Several months later, I shared with her a written plan for this project. She embraced it. We discussed creating a book that would explore autism from a unique vantage and reveal truths not commonly held.

The project was to be a collaboration of words and images capturing the essence of children dealing with autism.

I have been fortunate to share the joy of producing this book with Sharon and so many others who believed in the spirit of this project and contributed their love and support. Three very special people showed up just when we needed them. They made major contributions and sacrifices, giving their time, talent, expertise, and love. Without Craig and Alyson Beytien and Keith McPherson, this book would not have been possible. Our hearts were bound together in the shared belief that this book was needed and would touch many lives. This is our gift to the world, our legacy in the spirit of Leonardo.

I encourage you to take time to absorb the words and images. Visit the text again and again and look into the eyes of these beautiful children. It is my hope you will discover the true souls waiting to be revealed.

Thomas Balsamo

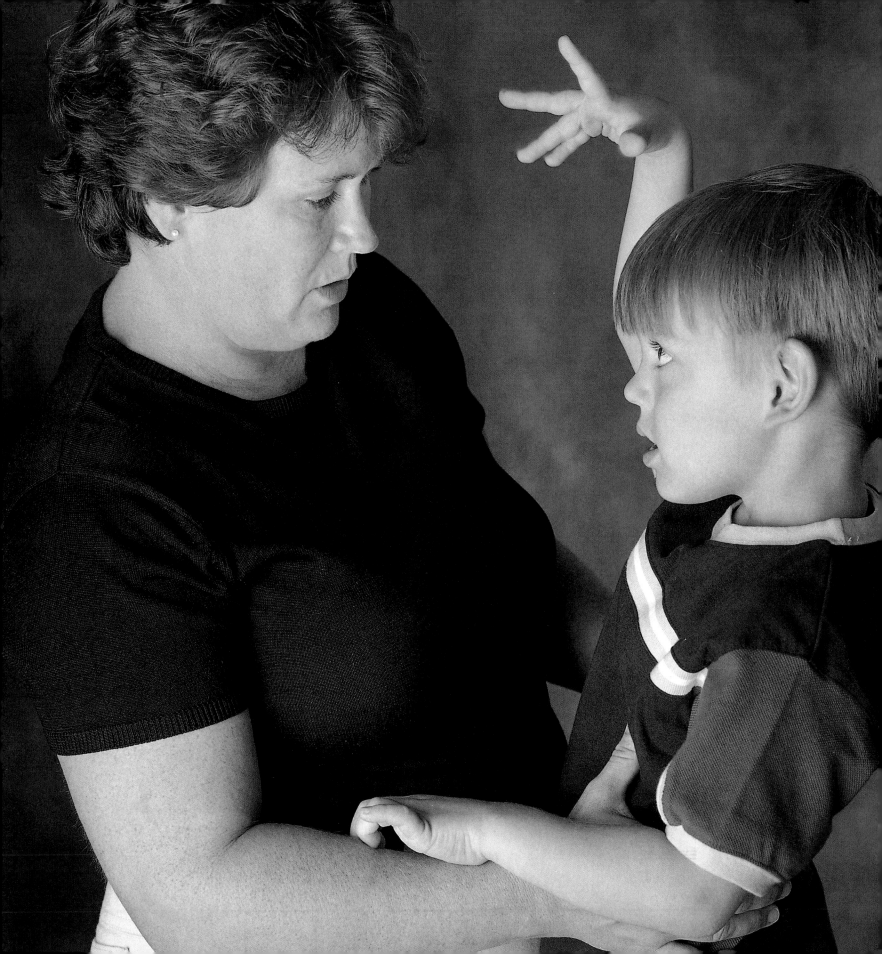

Table of Contents

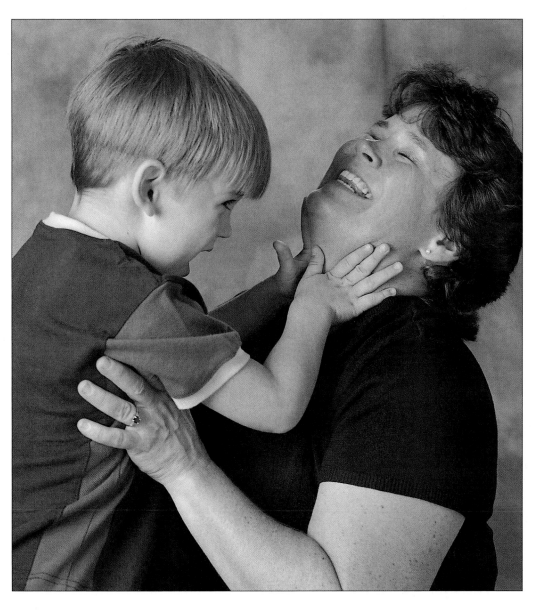

the dream

"HOW DO YOU MAKE GOD LAUGH?   TELL HIM YOUR PLANS."

Each of us creates a dream,
first for ourselves and then for our
children. While some of us are
architects with detailed plans,
others believe life simply sweeps us
along. In either case, consciously
and concrete or subconsciously
and subtle, we ultimately envision
ourselves as someone with our own
distinct destiny. And from that
vision, we choose our path in life.
For our children, either already
born or yet to be, we fancy
ourselves directors, taking cues
from their strengths and weaknesses
to mold the best "life performance"
possible. We often superimpose our
own dreams and wishes onto theirs,
almost as if we get a second chance
to "do it right" through them.

  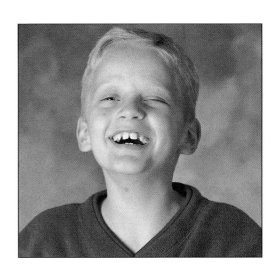

With the diagnosis of **autism**, the dream dies.

death in th

Death is a strong word.

It represents the removal of all hope.

It implies finality. For many parents,

the diagnosis of autism is a kind of

death. Professionals leave little or

no room for hope in a recognizable

form. Dreams wither and die while

the child remains, and "life" as we

know it comes to an end. To lower

the depth of misery, families are left

with what to do with this "person,"

this apparent shell destined to live

in a purgatory outside the boundaries

of the world in which we exist.

e diagnosis

The diagnosis removes the remaining wiggle room we create in hopes that this child could, and eventually would, some day be "normal." Those of us who parent a child with autism have stood quietly at their bedside, watching in wonder as they experience the first visible moments of peace in the twilight of sleep.

Caught up in the stillness, we imagine they will wake one day devoid of symptoms. We silently pray they will be one of the lucky ones we've heard about who "outgrow" their challenges. We envision a future where we laugh at the sheer folly of our former fears, for here before us stands a miraculously perfect human being. We picture the pain and anxiety associated with these earlier days becoming a distant memory, crowded out by newer ones filled with beautifully met developmental milestones. Dreams flood our minds in the form of soccer games and school plays, a sweaty child flushed with play running past us on the way to another adventure.

The diagnosis makes such moments of hope a luxury, yet we continue to indulge in the dream from time to time when pain cries out for relief.

Eventually, the price of such optimism is the crush of disappointment as time passes and our miracle fails to arrive. Waiting at the window we have been given where such transformations may occur, we feel hope slip slowly and silently away, each passing day the odds against it growing.

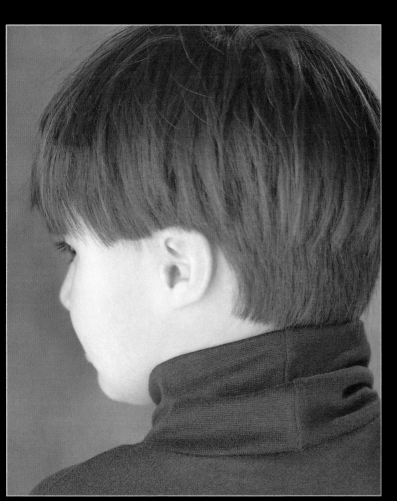

Driving away from the hospital, the day my child's future was erased, I was suddenly over-whelmed by the weight of reality and was unable to continue to drive. I turned the car into the drive-thru of a fast-food restaurant and ordered the obligatory fries and drink, handing them to the stranger who sat beside me silently strapped in his car seat.

In a moment of such intense pain, I feared I could not draw another breath, I wondered how I was to get this car and its occupant home. I have no way of knowing how long we sat there, engine idling, eyes fixed on some distant horizon. Time was suspended. Over and over I saw myself seated in front of the doctor, nodding as the death sentence was pronounced, trying to hear above the roar of the emotion flooding my ears. I heard the prognosis of never and always, words offering no place to hitch my dreams of recovery.

I watched myself respond to questions and gather my belongings, but how I got to the car and reached the drive-thru was a blur. Finally, with a jolt of adrenaline to prod me, I put the car in gear and somehow auto piloted us home, yet to have shed a tear.

Realities of such magnitude can only be experienced in small dosages. What happens between these moments of comprehension is an altered state of being.

Cars drive and doors open and shut. We speak and move about much as we once did; yet there's a surreal quality to our existence. Often, we find ourselves not breathing, air held until the tightness in our chest triggers its release. The sights and sounds around us seem to exist in a tunnel, no longer clear and visible as before. Shock has set in and defense mechanisms take over, allowing for meal preparation and the execution of duties. And if, by chance, life's spices invade our senses and we find ourselves caught up in a moment of laughter, hearts light and heads clear, we quickly learn that lurking behind us, poised to strike, is a reminder.

Like an adept thief, reality moves in stealth and is unpredictable. At the next table, we might catch a wisp of conversation between parent and child, an exchange so foreign and far-reaching from ones we've experienced, we are hit from behind and shoved face first back into the diagnosis, slapped back into submission.

There are episodes so clearly burned into memories we can play them back with perfect clarity, many years after they occur. On the day my son and I attended a neighborhood birthday party, the mood was festively chaotic with hordes of children, dressed in their finest, diving into presents and sweets as their mothers attempted conversation above the din. Caught up in revelry, no one noticed the child so clearly bewildered and distressed. Yet there, among his peers, my son was the personification of his diagnosis. Unable to relate or play, overwhelmed by the sights and sounds and desperate for removal, we slipped out the sliding door onto the deck. Hand on wrist I pulled him across the yard, chilled with panic and shame.

Somewhere near the swing set, my knees gave out and I felt the grass against my palms, stripped of defenses and reeling with the recognition of his limitations. There were no warning alarms sounding in my head that morning as I dressed him and kissed his face. I remember being mildly encouraged by his progress, when at breakfast he'd spontaneously asked for his juice, stringing two full words together. Yet here, in the arena of normalcy, his progress felt trivial and insignificant and my optimism seemed foolish in the face of comparison.

We don't remember days, we remember moments.

drowning on the surface of what is seen

I can remember waking from deep exhaustion, the type of sleep that almost hurts in its intensity, and coming up from a dream, as one swims frantically toward the surface, seeking air--at first rushing upward, then panicking as the light becomes closer and the depths of sleep give way to the start of the day. There, at the surface, was the challenge of the day, accompanied by the face of a child, desperate and always in need. It was there, on the surface, that I fought not to drown, not to be pulled down, barely catching my life's breath from yesterday, to face another day.

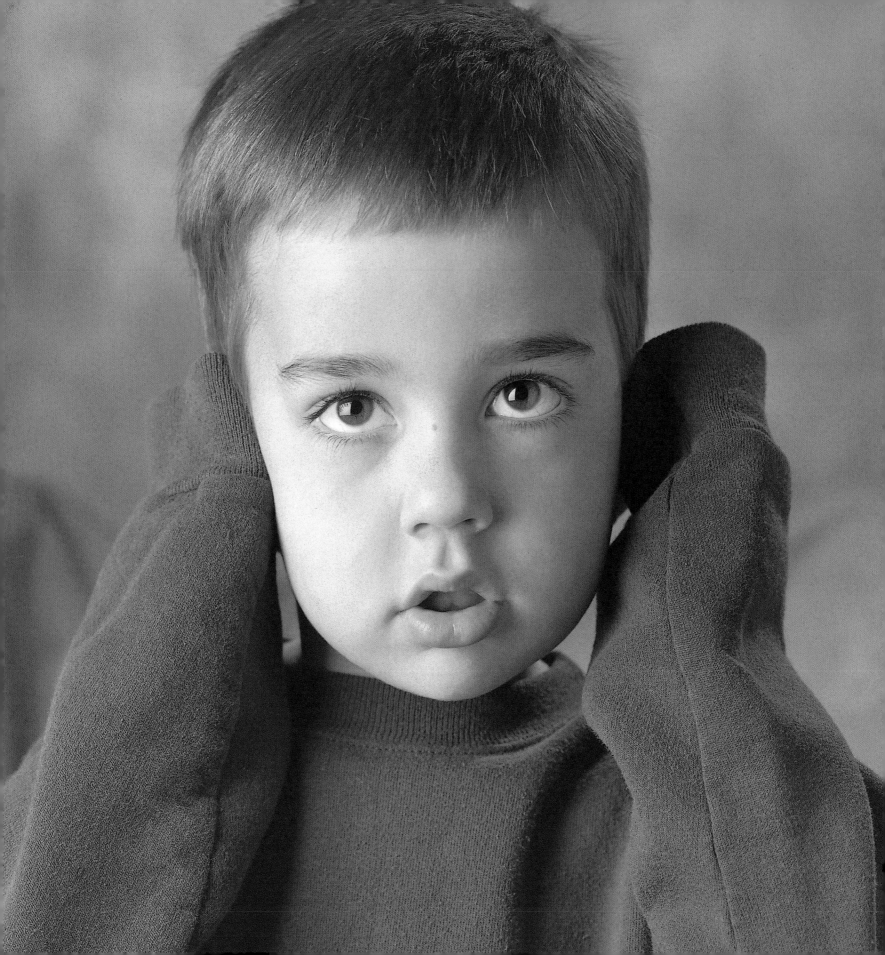

The desperate selfishness, the all-consuming and ravenous nature of this beast called autism can and will bring the strongest to their knees.

Often, the more one views what is familiar, the less they see what is hidden, crying out to be known. For those in the trenches of the day to day, or in the ivory towers of academia, that which manifests itself on the surface, in your face and ugly, is often *all* that is understood. The behavior becomes *who* the affected child is, rather than what he is trying to convey.

For within each of those who bear the label *autistic* lies a human trapped between our world and theirs, screaming to know and be known, often being taken for little more than their screams.

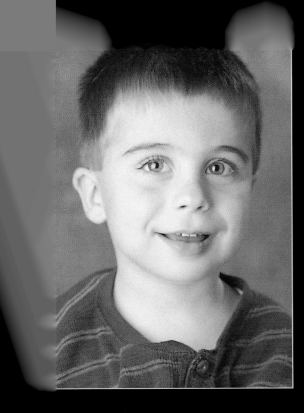
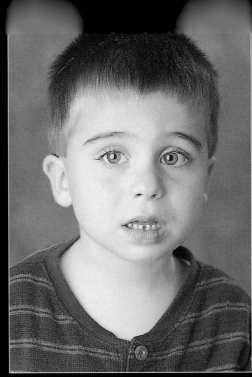
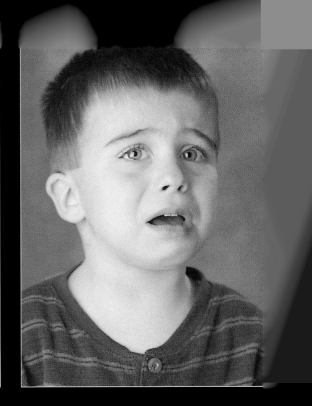

People with autism do not experience the world as others do. Each sense seems to hum on a different frequency. Their eyes, open or closed, do not see as we do.

While we may order the same meal, what they taste and touch is not on our plate. Einstein said he could never fully understand the concept of time. We watch the clock and agonize at how time is slow in waiting, only to slip through our fingers in times of rejoicing. Yet we possess an internal clock that serves us well. It allows comfort in the moment, as we come to understand early in life that one moment passes to

The clocks of autism do not automatically function with such features. People with autism often experience intensity without anticipation of relief. Transitions from moment to moment, from place to place, at the least are daunting and very often terrifying.

... people with autism

From this reality, we frequently see the world of the autistic colliding head-on with the one in which they are destined to live. Chaos and motion combine to create an atmosphere of "flight or fight." For those whose world revolves around the child with autism, survival is often the order of the day.

We clothe and feed, transport and chase, with the goal of simply getting everyone in our domain through the day, constantly battling the whirlpool of challenge that threatens to pull us under. Unlike those whose limitations are obvious, people with autism wear the mask of normalcy. Their faces do not betray the burden they carry, yet their actions invite rash judgment on themselves and those who tend to them.

The essence of autism defies the ordered design of our world, hence the person with autism becomes a victim of design, receiving the dual punishment of living with internal distress and being judged harshly for failing because of it.

wear the mask of normalcy.

In an effort to bring an autistic child out into the world while helping him learn the skills necessary to navigate through it, we are often faced with battling the world's perceptions. Boundaries and rules of engagement as we know them are mysteries to the person with autism.

After completing a nearly successful lunch with friends, I was attempting to steer my son out of a restaurant to the finish line of non-disaster. Almost to the door, he reached out his hand and touched a woman's wallet lying at her table's edge. Intercepting his grasp, I had almost whisked him out the door when the woman loudly announced her opinion that incompetent parents should refrain from bringing untrained brats into public. At this juncture in my life, I had yet to confess to a stranger my son's label, rather hoping I could help him pass the inspection of the world's watchful eye without the necessity of excusing him.

On this day, I had failed and was being called to stand red-faced before this judge and confess my son's flawed construction. No sooner did my admission and apology reach the victim than she declared she wasn't interested in my excuses, only that I think before bringing him out in public again. Arms flailing, I gasped for retorts and breath, while sinking into anger and despair, pulling my drowning child down with me.

In surviving, we discover

the soul's profound need to thrive.

Through grace-filled moments,

I caught glimpses of something in

my drowning child's eyes. I felt some-

thing flicker through his embrace that

beckoned me across the bridge to his

world, where once visited, we were

compelled to reach each other again

and again.

across the bri

Nothing of this world compares with

the embrace of a person with autism.

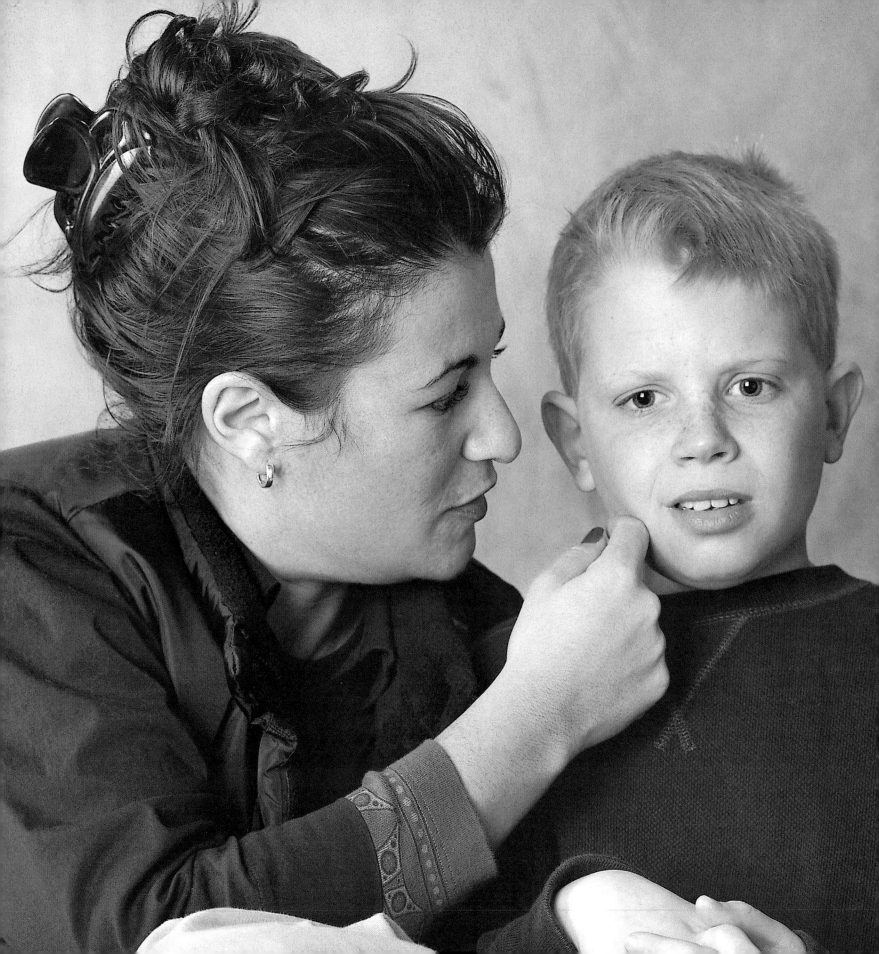

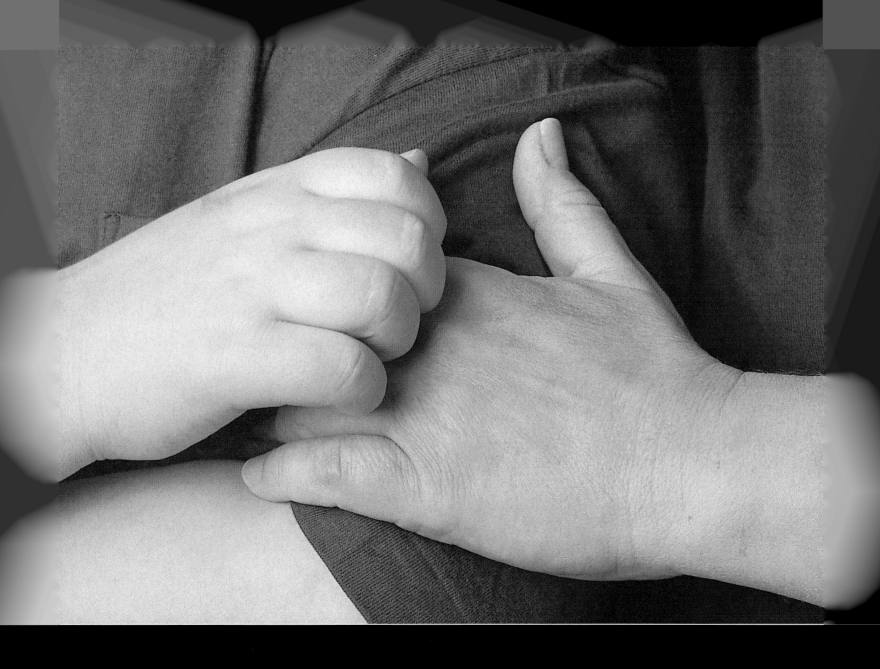

We touch often in our day, reaching out a hand to colleagues, hugging a friend. We peck cheeks when appropriate and hang our arm upon a shoulder from time to time. We know and understand the rules. Barely do we feel much beyond mild warmth associated with the exchange of human contact. Often, we feel nothing.

At a very young age, it was clear my child could not be handled in a typical way. My father was attempting to take him for a walk. Bewildered, and with a look of fear in his eyes I could not recall seeing before, my father asked why my son would not allow his hand to be touched, recoiling at every attempt.

Such reactions are inherent in the nature of a person with autism and, met with rejection or confusion, even those wanting to reach out often cease their attempts at contact. The autistic child with hands firmly clasped to their ears is not rejecting another's words, just the intensity of the volume, which causes pain.
In reality, their senses betray them. Their senses often fail to work together when providing information and lack the built-in filters we take for granted that allow us to tune out some of the information coming in and select only what we want and need to experience. Sights, sounds, and touch can be so overwhelming there is often the need to retreat to safer ground. Plagued with significant communication difficulties, others assume they lack desire to communicate.

These assumptions are erroneous and dangerous, for when we dehumanize any group, we allow ourselves the power to treat them in less-than-human ways.

Historically, these assumptions have been the cornerstone of the greatest atrocities known to humankind. Autism lends itself to such treatment. And the abyss created by these obstacles becomes the great divide between the person with autism and the rest of the world.

Autism places its victims across this divide and leaves them stranded without the tools to consistently return.

Rather than the two-way street of typical relationships, we encounter a narrow, single-lane bridge, one that often requires us to venture to the other side alone. Yet it is here on these journeys that we come to experience the exquisite joy of meeting the person and guiding them back. These profound moments of connection turn our notions of perfection upside down.

For here on the bridge, we experience humanness in its most pure and radiant form. So welcome is our embrace, so deep is the longing that exists within the individual, that the encounters can touch us more deeply than we have experienced before.

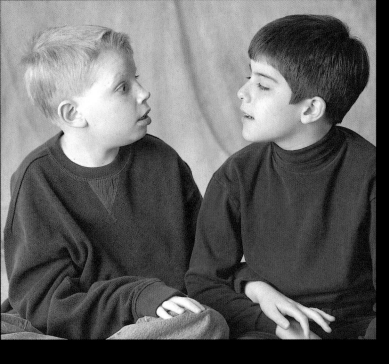

These moments are not exclusive to family members or those with strong investments in the individual with autism.

From peers to strangers, those who have dared to believe there is a person lurking beyond the prickly borders have returned moved, sometimes shaken, but never unchanged. These individuals, in such overriding distress over simply navigating life,

Those who have reached across the abyss that so often separates us from the autistic have discovered a humanness that in turn touches their very soul and beckons them to return again and again.

the redemption

It is written in many holy books that God will transform the world not with the mighty, but with the meek. Perhaps it is this ancient and universal truth that comes to light in the eyes of a person with autism. Their power of transformation gives witness to the quiet miracles they affect in the lives of those who touch and are touched by them.

I can only imagine what I am to become because of, not in spite of, my child with autism.

We are living in a culture that bombards our senses with the mantra that perfection is the key to happiness, the ultimate brass ring to be reached, fashioned from images that surround our very existence.

Messages are sent that if only we could achieve a bit more, do it better, and look marvelous while obtaining it, we would finally experience true joy. We are encouraged to clamor and climb the ladder of success, discarding anything that slows or hampers the ascent to heaven on earth. Perhaps what leads us so far astray from this goal of true happiness is our misguided conception of what perfection looks like.

We picture the aesthetics to resemble what we witness daily on screens and in print. And in our quest for utopia, we attempt to eliminate the flaws and the flawed. For surely no one invites pain and suffering into their life, and faced with even the mildly uncomfortable, we must find ways to rid ourselves of its burden so as not to disrupt our journey to a blissful existence.

Ultimately, when the elusive brass ring remains just beyond our grasp, we are prodded to pour more energy into the same pursuits, convinced that what prevents a sense of peace and completeness in our lives are the trials and tribulations that keep stepping in the way. And yet, as possessions and achievements stack higher and higher and the world continues to advance and prosper beyond our wildest imagination, we are often no closer to the destination we so covet.

For those who face the "forever" of autism, examination of the world's notions of perfection are impossible to avoid, for at every turn we risk being crushed by the failure of our children to achieve the world's standards of greatness. Our lives are more about surviving than thriving. Individuals with autism offer few opportunities to showcase that which our society prizes and seem to be the embodiment of what most would dread: An endless cycle of struggle and challenge, with no hope that the fruits of such labor will bear the seal of typical, let alone exemplary, lives.

Yet quietly and often through the profoundly simple, the children of autism rescue their caregivers from the depths of failure and despair while creating a different road, paved with smaller steps and unassuming achievements. All the while they give witness to the extraordinary miracles possible within our daily existence. Experiencing life with those in the world of autism gives us a different lens, lending new vision to everything we took for granted and hurried past on the way to notions of life's greater priorities. For as we bring the person with autism across the bridge time and again, we find that in our quest to orient them to our world, we are often the ones being transformed. As we become a guide for them, we find ourselves receiving remarkable insight into what truly nourishes our souls. The flash of a smile as they master a button or navigate the murky waters of a crowd, landing safely into our embrace, produce such aching joy, such moments of sheer delight that we experience and understand the world in a profoundly different way. And if we are inspired to do a victory dance over the acquisition of a simple task, it is not that we have been reduced to celebrating the paltry spoils of their

accomplishments, rather we more deeply appreciate the amazing gift inherent in even the smallest new connection they discover and recognize the vast distance they have traveled to get there.

I have found the paradox that if I love until it hurts, there is no hurt, only more love.
~Mother Theresa

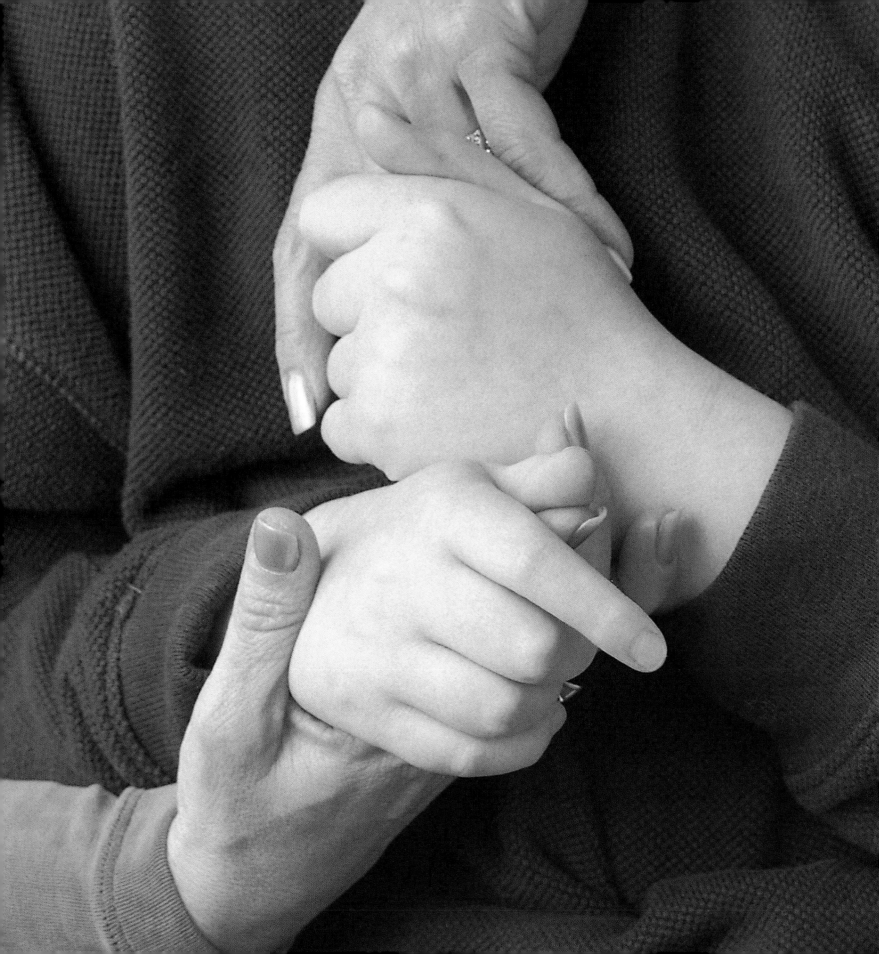

On an evening many months after my son's diagnosis, I fell absently into a chair, bleary from the day's labor and eager for the mindless diversion television might offer me. I found myself witnessing a story of a family's horrific tragedy and suffering. In an instant I was weeping, not the misty-eyed trickle of tears one might shed witnessing a sad scene, but waves of anguish accompanied by outward cries of pain.

There I sat, incapable of stemming the floodgates that had been spontaneously torn open in an unguarded moment of empathy. My heart had ripped apart, pouring forth tears of grief that my flimsy walls of denial had contained for so long. Witnessing the pain of another family had inadvertently released a wellspring of tears as I mourned for my son. Yet somehow tethered to my brokenness was an insight into the sufferings of others.

In that moment, I glimpsed the reality that the capacity to experience such pain was universal, and I was not alone. I knew then that my heart had broken open. What I could not yet comprehend was how that brokenness would make room for so much and so many.

The beauty of hindsight is in seeing where the journey has brought you. In the raw space that was now my heart, a world of connection had opened to me. And in each encounter with those in the autism trenches, or in the chance encounters with a stranger who offered a glimpse into their struggle on life's difficult roads, I experienced meetings of both heart and mind. I found myself stepping into the sanctuary of another's soul as we shared a true and profound intimacy in the exquisite grace such moments allow.

Nowhere in the acquisition of accomplishments and accolades had anything given me the sense of pride and deep inner peace my altered perspective now revealed.

The person with autism is both teacher and guide, bringing us back to a place where over and over we experience moments of pure happiness. Their lessons, while hard-earned, transform the very way in which we experience others in our lives. For when my daughter toddled into the kitchen just shy of her second birthday, having fully dressed by her own design, I could not help but marvel at the miracle her accomplishment represented. And as I held her tightly in my arms, spinning her in wonder and joy, I did not mourn the painstaking steps I had endlessly repeated, my hands firmly clasped over my son's, as I taught his fingers the sequence of pulling a sock onto his foot.

Rather, the contrast allowed me to celebrate the gift my daughter and her milestones of normalcy truly were, while being brought to my knees in triumph and gratitude at seeing a sock, heel side up, resting proudly on my boy's toes.

Bedtime rituals inspire both reflection and closure as we gauge the day's successes while attempting to put failures to rest. On a cold night many years ago, I added a blanket to my son's bed and prepared to close the chapter on another day. Feeling only weariness and the dull ache of guilt, I scrolled back and took inventory. Was I doing enough? Had I made the right choices? In a life filled with schedules and symbols, therapists and interventions, I was a novice sailor with no compass to direct me. Tucking the blanket under his chin, I stared into his eyes. A mixture of deep love and stabbing fear rushed over me. I placed my lips against his forehead and lingered there, a sigh intermingling with the kiss. As I walked away, the silence was broken by my son's voice calling after me.

So often, I felt like Annie Sullivan pumping water over Helen Keller's hands while signing the word water. Desperate to pair meaning with language, I repeatedly poured the words of my heart over him, only to have them echoed back without apparent comprehension.

Yet on this night, the burdens of struggle and self-doubt fell away as I turned back to see a radiant smile lighting up my son's face. And there I received my guiding star: the words "I love you so much, Mrs. Mom" for the very first time.

the souls

People with autism do not live by the rules of the world they were born into.

It is from this reality that we stand in awe at what profound lessons each are capable of teaching. They see a reality our larger picture of life does not allow us to view. The absence of social programming, cultural conditioning, and all that prejudices everything we taste, touch, and see gives people with autism the closest thing to God's eyes we have here on Earth.

Friendship is the intricate balance of give and take, of chemistry, proximity, and mystery.

The possibilities are infinite, the true ones rare.

The only characteristic consistent in each true friendship is that it is mutual. There must always be two. Friendship is a bridge between islands and the promise of relief from isolation. The desire to share both time and heart runs deep within us all.

In developing friendships, energy flows both ways. We must be nourished in order to nourish. Friendships grow and die. And while we may love and be loved often in our lifetime, for someone with autism, such love is not merely a spice of life. It is the food that allows them to grow.

With respect to autism, the challenges of the social aspects of life are frequently addressed and lamented. The rules of engagement often escape even the most brilliant individual with autism. Unlike the rest of humankind who use measures such as time spent together, age, and a litany of criteria to rank and classify their circle of intimates, people with autism neither understand such systems nor care to oblige. Their friendships are not influenced by what someone wears, whom they vote for, or how they score on tests. They are not interested in a person based on religion or race or whether they are rich or poor. Individuals with autism are simply not influenced by one's exterior life.

For the rest of us, the challenge to achieve such purity of heart is seldom achieved.

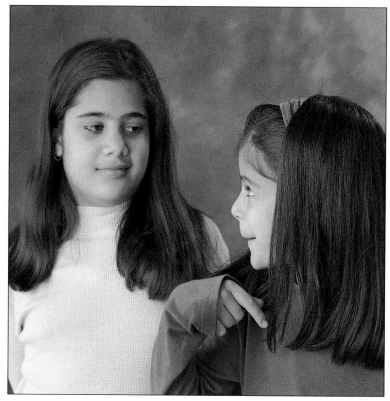

Being friends with an individual with autism means being loved for the very essence of who we are: The person that lies deep beneath layers of physical and social trappings.

The privacy of façades will fail to conceal true feelings from them, and we are often left with a sense of having been glimpsed behind our social masks.

Being loved by someone with autism is a cherished and coveted experience perhaps because when loved, we are linked to him or her in a manner that transcends surface layers.

It is the memory of connection, etched on the autistic heart, that earns us their friendship. And no amount of time or space will alter their feelings. With this remarkable and purest of bonds, we come away feeling eternally blessed.

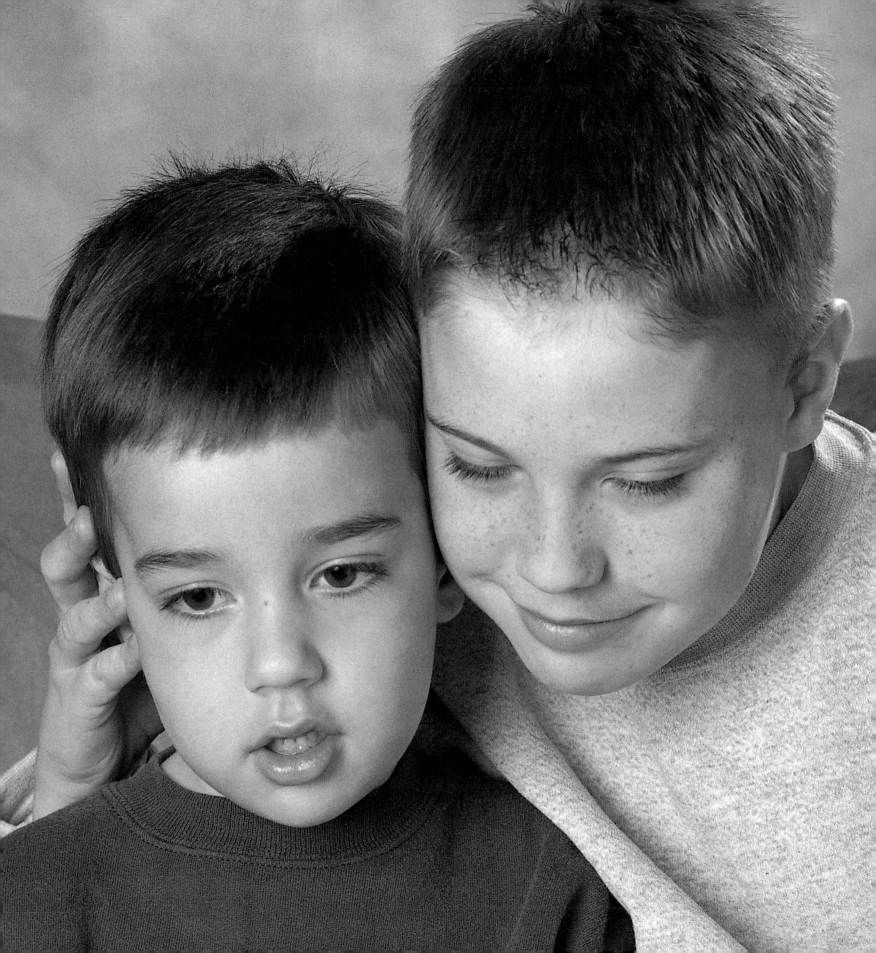

The maintenance engineer at my son's school was an object of loathing and fear. Eternally gruff, he menaced the students with his angry glare and quick reprimands. The staff was no more endeared to him, and if he captured their attention at all, it prompted speculations as to his mental stability and possible vices. What drew my son to him no one could guess. Yet each day, in the midst of peers and chaos, my son sought him out for a greeting. This unlikely pair met daily, and the anger in the man's eyes was said to soften with my son's approach. I happened upon them in an empty hallway one afternoon, walking side by side engaged in some semblance of conversation. I was moved by the respectful way the man tilted his head toward my son's banter, allowing him the repetition of his social phrases.

Once my son had returned to class, I introduced myself and thanked him for his role in my son's school day. I explained that he was mentioned frequently at home, and my son considered him a cherished friend. With this, the man's eyes filled with tears. Embarrassed, he turned his face away and mumbled how hearing that had just made his day. As I walked away, he called after me. In a voice breaking with emotion, he told me hearing that had just made his year.

I have come to know, contrary to popular myth, that the person with autism has a profound capacity for emotional attachment and feelings.

However deep my maternal instincts may run, no matter the countless affirmations I may have received from those who love someone with autism, the burden of proof has fallen to those of us considered too emotionally attached to assess such capacities. Fear would creep into my mind that the world might somehow use the idea of people with autism having less-than-human capacities for feeling as a  weapon against them. And the deep, unabiding and unconditional love I knew my son and those in the autistic world were feeling could be shrugged off as simply a wishful notion.

When faith and reason occur in tandem, the results are often spectacular. The recent use of sophisticated neuroimaging has given us the first glimpses into active human brains and has opened a window to the ultimate inner sanctum. In the sterile confines of the laboratory, the autistic mind has been analyzed and mapped. The studies confirm with neuromagnetic pictures what scientists had long been purporting: Autistic brains don't react to facial cues the way normal brains do.

Upon further exploration, however, the academic world received data that would forever challenge long-held theories regarding the autistic and their capacity for relationships. When faces of strangers were replaced by faces of loved ones, the autistic brain "lights up like an explosion of Roman candles." In science's most sophisticated arena, those who share the sacred bonds of connection to people with autism-- those living, loving, and laughing with these extraordinary people day after day-- could finally view what was etched in the depths of the autistic soul: The capacity for love existing in a magnitude no boundaries of challenge could ever contain.

On the journey of life, what more do we really need to know?

Acknowledgments

*From its inception, this project has been blessed. The making of **Souls: Beneath and Beyond Autism** is a beautiful witness to the power of God's grace, and we are humbled and awed.*

From the families who ventured into the studio for photo sessions to the people in our daily existence who provided essentials in both word and deed, we abundantly received more than we would have dared to hope for. The bonds formed through participation in the creation of the book are deep and extraordinary. While we sought to create a gift, we ultimately received more than we gave and came away from this journey altered and eternally blessed.

A simple thanks does not adequately express the depth of our gratitude. Each person brought an integral piece to the project— most important, the gift of self. This outpouring of support provided both the inspiration and the momentum that took us from a dream to reality.

Craig and Alyson Beytien have shared many aspects of their lives, from the professional to the deeply personal, helping shape the very essence of the book.

Craig served as creative guide, challenging us to reach far beyond the superficial. As editor, he truly inspired the voice and helped liberate the message. He raised the bar, always believing a universal message could be found in the lives of autistic children.

Alyson's response to the work set the standard as we attempted to create a truth about autism and those who exist in its world. Her combination of knowledge and love was at the center of the collective heart behind the text's voice.

Keith McPherson epitomizes the spirit of this book. As the designer he became our conductor, combining the lyric of words and the music of images to create a work of art. Beyond talent, he shared the beauty and tenderness of his heart, and its essence is felt on each page.

Joyce Balsamo and Bob Rosenbloom are the ideal life partners. Their inspiration and personal sacrifice was pivotal in this project's inception and completion. From planting the seed to create a book, to her encouragement and input on its development, Joyce believed in the vision. Bob's endless enthusiasm and commitment to providing support were manifestations of his extraordinary selflessness. His life gives witness to love expressed through unconditional giving and joyous celebration in his family's triumphs.

Our children, Nickolas, Wade, and Michael Balsamo and Joey and Raia Rosenbloom, were the undercurrent that continually fueled our passion to take an ideal and make it a reality. Our infinite and boundless love for them inspired us to create a tangible record of the beliefs we hope to instill in their hearts and minds.

From our families, we received gifts that took root and bloomed in this book. Joe Kaminsky inspired relentless optimism and spirituality, combined with a deep desire to express the heart through words.

Carole Kaminsky gave the unwavering love, patience, and fierce maternal instincts that allowed for risks to be taken on behalf of children. When we faltered, Steve Kaminsky offered cathartic laughter, helping release the grip of despair long enough for our optimism to take hold again.

Sonia Dickson exemplifies dedication, a sheer force of will and unconditional love, witnessing their power in the life of a child.

Andy Valskis has been a true brother, envisioning the layout of the book and helping the words and images come together for the first time.

Virginia Balsamo instilled a desire to dream, and Joseph Balsamo exemplified the work ethic necessary to attain those dreams.

Treasured friendships continually refreshed our spirit with love and prayers, lifting us up when our strength failed us.

The staff of Portraits by Thomas kept the studio running, allowing time to be spent on *Souls* and also giving time and talent to the project:

Kara Roach

Jesse Cordova

Kim Fitzner

Sarah Renick

Sue Hartman

Lynn Wilson

Suzie Bishop

Danielle Pervey poured her energy and enthusiasm into the web site, www.booksthattouch.com

Heartfelt appreciation for providing essential support at the perfect time goes to:

Bill Graft and Charles Curtis
of Graft, Jordan & Curtis
Attorneys at Law

Jeannie Gilson

Sharon Stober
of Your Stepfamily Magazine

LeJane Carson
of Carson Stoga Communications

The folks at McGraw-Hill were quite generous in providing services donated or at cost to allow our vision to take form.

We're indebted to Ed Stanford, president of McGraw-Hill Higher Education, who supported this project from its inception. Cheryl Horch masterfully negotiated the production process for us, and Jess Kosic kindly copyedited the manuscript. Special thanks to Erwin Llererza for creating such a beautiful DVD for group presentations. The authors also thank Peggy Meidell, Bob Bolick, and Jennifer Perillo at McGraw-Hill for helping to make Souls available through McGraw-Hill.

We express appreciation to Quebecor World, ProGraphics, Inc., and Phoenix Color Corporation for their support and assistance. We would also like to thank McGraw-Hill Corporate Manufacturing, for donating the paper.

A hug to Ellen Gaspari for sharing the first tear that set the dream in motion.

And ultimately, we thank the children and families who gave us the extraordinary opportunity to enter their world and capture a glimpse for others to view.

The faces, stories, and words of each family were in our hearts and minds, every moment of the book's creation:

The Belrose Family

The Beytien Family

The Bickner Family

The Bock Family

The Brady Family

The Cabin Family

The Fenlon-Panozzo Family

The Gaspari Family

The Gay Family

The Hallman Family

The Hoffman Family

The Hofmeister Family

The Jethwa Family

The Kessler Family

The Lewis Family

The Lindberg Family

The Mahn Family

The Morgan Family

The Nachtwey Family

The Nihill Family

The Partridge Family

The Pilafas Family

The Planera Family

The Reed Family

The Rosenbloom Family

The Royko Family

The Shields Family

The Sieger Family

The Thompson Family

The Wiebe Family

The Williams Family

The Wirth Family

Thomas Balsamo

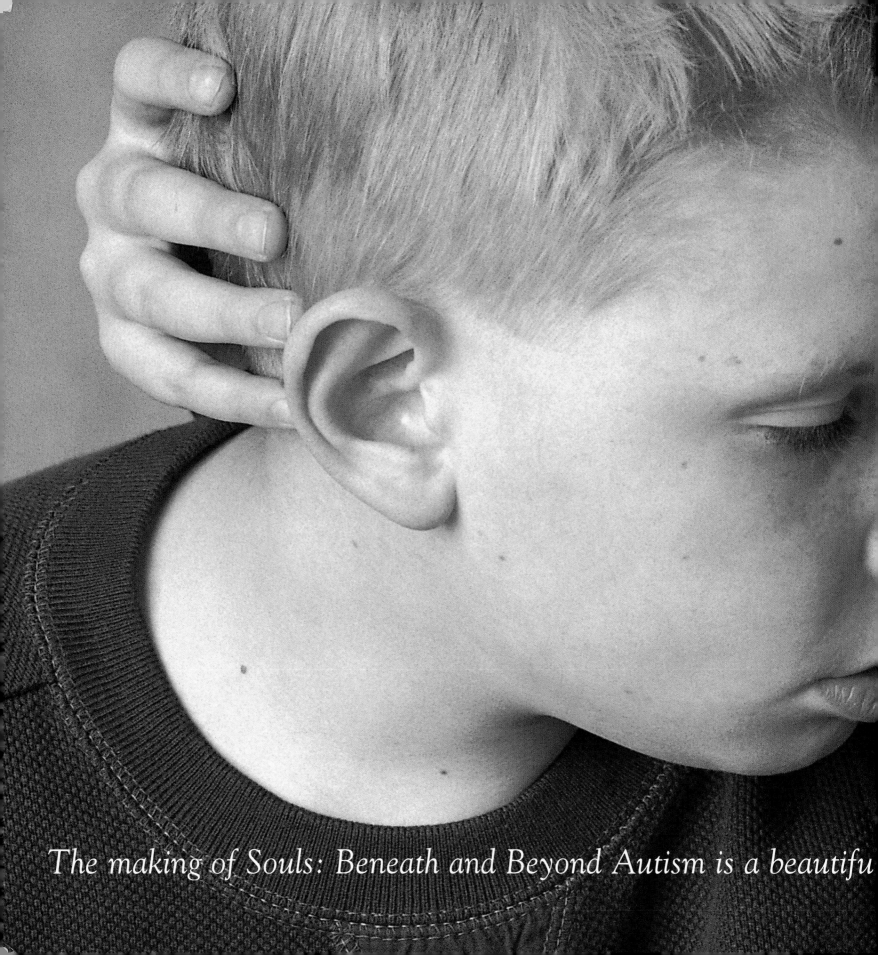

The making of Souls: Beneath and Beyond Autism is a beautifu

witness to the power of God's grace, and we are humbled and awed.